Who W
Kobe Bryant?

Who Was Kobe Bryant?

by Ellen Labrecque

illustrated by Gregory Copeland

Penguin Workshop

To my friends and former colleagues
at *Sports Illustrated Kids* magazine—who
were there for the Kobe years—EL

PENGUIN WORKSHOP
An Imprint of Penguin Random House LLC, New York

Copyright © 2020 by Penguin Random House LLC. All rights reserved.
Published by Penguin Workshop, an imprint of Penguin Random House LLC, New York.
PENGUIN and PENGUIN WORKSHOP are trademarks of Penguin Books Ltd.
WHO HQ & Design is a registered trademark of Penguin Random House LLC.
Printed in the USA.

Visit us online at www.penguinrandomhouse.com.

Library of Congress Cataloging-in-Publication Data is available upon request.

ISBN 9780593225707 (paperback)   10 9 8 7 6 5 4 3 2 1
ISBN 9780593225714 (library binding)   10 9 8 7 6 5 4 3 2 1

Contents

Who Was Kobe Bryant?

It was June 26, 1996, the night of the National Basketball Association—the NBA—draft, when professional teams select new players. Wearing a dark suit on his slim six-foot, six-inch frame, Kobe Bryant, seventeen, was waiting for his name to be called. Just days earlier, Kobe had graduated from Lower Merion High School outside of Philadelphia, Pennsylvania. He was considered the best high-school basketball player in the nation. High-school players usually went to college to prepare themselves for entering the NBA draft. Kobe was different. He wanted to become a professional right away.

"Playing in the NBA has been my dream since I was three," Kobe said.

The Philadelphia 76ers—Kobe's hometown

team—had the first pick in the draft. They chose Allen Iverson from Georgetown University. The first twelve teams all chose college players. Finally, the Charlotte Hornets selected Kobe with the thirteenth pick.

Once his name was announced, Kobe put on a Hornets baseball cap before he walked to the podium to greet the TV cameras.

Kobe, though, would never play one minute for the Hornets. Even as he smiled in front of the cameras, Charlotte was already talking with the Los Angeles Lakers about trading Kobe for an experienced center, Vlade Divac. The Hornets, with number thirteen, had a much higher pick than the Lakers, who had the twenty-fourth selection. Charlotte chose somebody who would be a valuable trade for Los Angeles. The Hornets already had all-stars who played shooting guard, Kobe's position. They wanted someone like the seven-foot-one-inch-tall Divac.

Kobe was grinning on the outside, but the details of the draft would stick with him. The fact that twelve—really thirteen—teams had passed on him would fuel his drive to be the best for the next twenty years.

Kobe did become one of the NBA's greatest players of all time. He won five NBA titles, led the league in scoring two times, and was an eighteen-time All-Star.

But on the day of the 1996 NBA draft, seventeen-year-old Kobe still had his whole career in front of him—and he was ready to play.

CHAPTER 1
A Kid Named Kobe

Kobe Bryant was born on August 23, 1978, in Philadelphia, Pennsylvania. His first name came from a type of Japanese beef that his parents had noticed on a restaurant menu. Kobe's mom, Pamela, said later they always knew their son would be special, and that is why they choose that unique name. Kobe's dad, Joe Bryant, was a professional basketball player for the 76ers.

When Kobe was three, he loved to watch his dad play on television. While he watched, Kobe would often run down the hallway, jump onto a mini trampoline, and slam a ball into an eight-foot-high plastic hoop.

When Kobe was six, his dad's basketball career

changed his family's lives. Joe had played for eight seasons and had been traded to two different teams. In 1983, he moved his whole family to Rieti, Italy, so he could play basketball there. Rieti is a small city fifty miles from Rome.

The Bryant family did not know how to speak Italian at first. Kobe had two older sisters,

Kobe with his basketball team in Italy

Sharia and Shaya, and they spent afternoons teaching each other the language. Eventually Kobe spoke Italian as well as he spoke English.

Joe's team had its own youth squad that Kobe joined. Despite being so young, Kobe's skills stood out right away. His talent might have come from his dad, but his personality came from his mother.

Pam was the stern one in the family. Kobe hardly ever smiled when he played. "He was always so serious about everything he did as far as sports," said his sister Sharia.

Kobe's father switched teams every few years while playing in Italy. No matter where they moved, Kobe always found a place to play basketball.

Kobe's grandfather, Grandpa Cox, still lived in the United States. He recorded NBA games on his television, boxed up the tapes, and sent them to his grandson. Kobe watched the games again and again. He studied the moves of NBA players like Michael Jordan of the Chicago Bulls. Then he would go to the courts near his house and practice those moves for hours at a time.

In November 1991, when Kobe was thirteen, his family returned to Philadelphia. He was back in his home country, but he felt like an outsider. He didn't understand American slang. He didn't know what clothes were cool to wear. Kobe didn't blend in with the kids at school. He took the anger he felt about being an outsider, and he used it on the basketball court.

The year after he returned to the United States, Kobe attended Lower Merion High School. He started on the varsity basketball team as a freshman and spent every free second practicing. In addition to his high-school team, Kobe played on an Amateur Athletic Union (AAU) team. They played against all-star teams from all over the country. During the summer, Kobe attended top basketball camps and faced other great players. He began to stand out, even among the best.

Kobe "worked harder than any other kid I've ever seen," said Sam Rines, one of Kobe's coaches.

By the time Kobe was a senior, he was considered to be the best high-school player in the entire country.

During his senior season, Kobe led Lower

Merion to a state-championship title and averaged more than thirty points and twelve rebounds per game. Almost every college basketball team in the country recruited him.

On April 29, 1996, Kobe held a news conference in his high-school gym. Photographers, writers, teammates, and friends surrounded him. Everybody wanted to hear Kobe's decision. He announced, "I've decided to skip college and take my talent to the NBA." The crowd erupted in cheers. Kobe flashed a bright grin.

CHAPTER 2
Welcome to the Show

Less than a month after Kobe joined the Los Angeles Lakers, Shaquille O'Neal left the Orlando Magic and also signed with the Lakers. Standing at seven feet, one inch and weighing more than three hundred pounds, Shaq was the most dominating center in the world.

Kobe's first season in the NBA (1996–1997) was a learning experience. He was much younger than his teammates. This made it difficult for him to fit in with them. When they traveled, he sat quietly on the plane, watching movies or reading. He spent a lot of time alone in his hotel room, ordering room service and watching other NBA games. In the playoffs, the Lakers were losing three games to one against the Utah Jazz in the second round of a best-of-seven-game series. If the Lakers lost Game Five, their season was finished. The game was tied 87–87 with eleven seconds to go. Kobe took the Lakers' final shot—it was an air ball, a completely missed shot. The game went into overtime, and things only got worse for Kobe. He shot three more air balls, and his team lost. The Lakers' season was over.

The team flew home from Utah to California that night. His teammates were disappointed and exhausted. But Kobe was already planning for the next season. The moment he stepped off the plane, he drove to a high school down the street from his house. A janitor opened the gym for him. Kobe shot baskets all night. When the sun came up, he kept shooting. He never wanted to let down his teammates or his fans again.

Kobe spent the entire off-season working to improve. He played in the Lakers' summer league, lifted weights, worked with a trainer, and shot baskets endlessly. His hard work paid off. In his second season, he became the youngest player ever to start in the NBA All-Star game. During the game, he played against his idol, Michael Jordan. He challenged Michael, but he also asked him for advice and tips. Michael treated him like a little brother.

In Kobe's third season (1998–1999), he started every game and became the Lakers' second-leading scorer (behind Shaq). He also became a great defensive player by studying his opponents. At times, it seemed like Kobe knew what move a player was going to make before the player did.

Shaquille O'Neal (1972–)

Shaquille O'Neal was born in Newark, New Jersey. He is one of the greatest big men ever to play in the NBA. He played like a wrecking ball, knocking down anybody who got in his way and giving himself nicknames like Superman and Shaq Fu.

Shaq was in the NBA for nineteen seasons (1992–2011) and won four NBA titles (three with the Lakers, one with the Miami Heat). He was as big of a deal off the basketball court as he was on it. Shaq starred in movies, made rap albums, and endorsed many products. Today he stars on *Inside the NBA*, a TV show where he talks about the game and its players.

During Kobe's fourth season, he and Shaquille led the Lakers to the 2000 NBA title. The Lakers had a new coach named Phil Jackson. Phil had coached Michael Jordan in Chicago, and he brought out the best in both Shaq's and Kobe's games. Under Phil, the Lakers repeated as champions the following season, in 2001. Kobe also married his girlfriend, Vanessa Laine, that spring.

The Lakers won a third title in 2002. Kobe and Shaquille were the perfect combination together on the court. Kobe was an awesome shooter from the outside and could beat any defender when he drove to the basket. He made dunks that were so high-flying and acrobatic that it looked like he was performing an Olympic gymnastics routine. Shaq was an unstoppable force underneath the hoop. His dunks rattled the backboards. With every championship, though, the relationship between Kobe and

Shaq became more complicated. They were teammates, but they were also rivals. Now that Kobe was a superstar, he didn't want to share the spotlight, or the ball, with another teammate. Kobe didn't want to play with Shaq anymore.

CHAPTER 3
Winning—at What Cost?

In January 2003, Kobe and Vanessa had a daughter, Natalia. Kobe loved being a husband, but when Vanessa gave birth to their daughter, he discovered that he especially loved being a dad. The family lived in a large house near the beach outside of Los Angeles.

Life was good for Kobe. The Lakers had won three straight NBA titles. He had earned hundreds of millions of dollars by playing for the Lakers and wearing Adidas sneakers. (Although he eventually moved from the Adidas brand to Nike.) He seemed to have it all. But Kobe was not always a good teammate. He was accused of being a ball hog. And when things went wrong on the court, he blamed the players around him. When the Lakers traveled, Kobe still didn't talk much or joke around. He was so brilliant at basketball at such a young age that he never understood the value of his teammates.

The Lakers' championship streak came to an end when they lost in the NBA Western Conference Semifinals in May 2003. After the season ended, Kobe flew to Vail, Colorado, for knee surgery. While in Colorado, he was accused of sexual assault by a hotel employee where he was staying. He was charged with a crime and, if convicted, he could have been sentenced to years in prison. Kobe said he was innocent.

While the case against him proceeded, Kobe continued to play basketball. But his life was turned upside down. During games, fans booed him every time he touched the ball. He flew back and forth between Los Angeles and Colorado to appear in court. His relationship with Shaq worsened. Kobe said that he either wanted Shaq to get traded, or *he* wanted to be traded. In the summer of 2004, the Lakers listened to Kobe. They traded Shaq to the Miami Heat.

In September 2004, the sexual-assault case against Kobe was dropped. The woman who had accused him didn't want the attention of testifying against him in public. Kobe made a public apology to her, and he agreed to pay her a settlement—an agreed-upon amount of money—so that he would not have to go back to court. He once again focused all his time and energy on basketball. He was now the Lakers' biggest star. He was determined to prove he could lead the team to a championship—all by himself.

CHAPTER 4
A New Man

Over the next five seasons, Kobe got everything he wanted as a player. Or, at least everything he *thought* he wanted. In the 2005–2006 and the 2006–2007 seasons, Kobe

led the league in scoring. On January 22, 2006, he scored eighty-one points in a game against the Toronto Raptors. It is the second-highest point total by a player in an NBA game ever.

Some critics, though, still thought Kobe was selfish and shot too much.

While Kobe continued to pile up individual accomplishments, his team failed in the playoffs. The Lakers made it to the 2008 NBA championship, but they lost to the Boston Celtics, four games to two. As each season ended without another championship trophy, Kobe became more frustrated. Making matters worse for Kobe, Shaq and the Miami Heat had won the 2006 NBA title, proving that Shaq didn't need Kobe to be a champion.

Kobe still spent much of his time alone. Rather than talk with teammates when flying home after a game, he studied the game on video to review his performance.

In 2008, the Summer Olympics were held in Beijing, China. Kobe was one of twelve NBA players selected for the US men's basketball team. The squad included some of the other best players in the world, including LeBron James of the Cleveland Cavaliers and Dwyane Wade of the Miami Heat. Kobe, who was turning thirty years old that summer, was the most experienced player on the team.

He had never played in the Olympics before, and the pressure on him and the rest of the US team to win the gold medal was huge. At first, critics predicted Kobe would hurt his squad with his "me first" attitude. Kobe proved them wrong. He impressed his teammates by how hard he worked. When the rest of the team was just arriving for their first practice, they found Kobe on the court dripping with sweat. He had already finished two workouts.

"That's when I knew he was a different beast," Dwyane Wade said about Kobe. "His example inspired me and other members of the team."

When the games started, Kobe shared the ball with his teammates and played some of the toughest defense of his career. He wasn't the team's leading scorer, but when the team needed

him to score—he did. In the championship game against Spain, Kobe scored thirteen points in the fourth quarter. The US team won the gold medal!

US Men's Olympic Basketball Team, 2008

Kobe now knew if he was going to win the NBA championship again, he had to challenge *and* encourage his teammates. He began to act like a leader. He offered advice to the younger players. He took the team out to dinner. But Kobe also insisted they work and practice as hard as he did. A couple of years earlier, Kobe had given himself a nickname—the Black Mamba—after the most dangerous snake in the world. He wanted his team to attack every opponent the way the black mamba goes after prey: deadly and fast. He urged his teammates to play with serious looks on their faces, not smiles. He wanted them to play the game like it was war.

Opponents and even teammates might not have liked Kobe's leadership style—but they respected it because it worked. In 2009, Los Angeles returned to the NBA Finals and defeated the Orlando Magic, four games to one.

The next season, Kobe hit six game-winning shots. It was the most by a player in one season in ten years. The Lakers repeated as champions in 2010, beating their longtime rivals, the Boston Celtics, four games to three. Kobe was named the most valuable player in both the 2009 and 2010 NBA Finals.

CHAPTER 5
Father Time Is Undefeated

The summer Kobe won his fifth NBA title, he turned thirty-two years old. After playing in the NBA for fourteen seasons, he no longer had anything to prove. He was considered an all-time great.

Kobe, though, was wearing down. His whole body ached from all the jumping and running that he had done over the years.

On April 7, 2013, the Lakers played the Golden State Warriors. In the fourth quarter of the game, Kobe drove to the basket but crumpled to the floor when he was fouled. He could not run and could barely stand. But before he left the game, he took two foul shots and made both, tying the score.

The thirty-four-year-old had torn his Achilles tendon—the tissues that connect the heel to the calf muscles. Kobe needed surgery, but he was still determined to play again. He approached his recovery the same way he approached basketball—intensely. He worked day and night to get stronger. Kobe returned to the Lakers after only seven months. Unfortunately, his comeback only lasted six games before he was injured again—this time with a broken kneecap.

The Lakers star faced one injury after another over the next couple of seasons. There is a saying in sports that "Father Time is undefeated." All athletes, no matter how great, eventually reach the age when they aren't as great as they once were. When Kobe was thirty-seven years old, he realized it was time to say goodbye to basketball.

On November 29, 2015, Kobe announced

plans to retire at the end of the 2015–2016 season. During his final year, he averaged just over seventeen points a game, and the Lakers finished last in the Western Conference. Kobe had played twenty seasons in the league—

all in Los Angeles. His final game was on April 13, 2016. After the game, Kobe spoke to the fans and thanked them for all their support. He ended his speech by saying, "Mamba out."

After Kobe retired, his life was still busy. He ran his own entertainment production company, called Granity Studios. He wrote an animated short film called *Dear Basketball.* It won an Academy Award in 2018. He created a book series for young adults called The Wizenard Series—it is a fantasy series set in the sports world.

Kobe also opened up the Mamba Sports Academy, a training facility for young athletes.

The best part of Kobe's retirement from basketball was that he got to spend more time with his family. By January 2020, he and Vanessa had four daughters: Natalia, seventeen; Gianna (who was called Gigi), thirteen; Bianka, three; and Capri, seven months. He loved being a father. Kobe said his second daughter, Gigi, was most like him. She was a fierce competitor who wanted to play college basketball and star in the Women's

National Basketball Association (WNBA). Kobe coached Gigi's team, the Mamba Lady Mavericks, which was run through his Mamba Sports Academy.

On January 26, 2020, Kobe, Gigi, and other players on the team and their families took off in a helicopter on their way to the Mamba Lady Mavericks basketball game. Kobe often traveled by helicopter during his NBA career, and he continued to fly during his retirement to save time.

The sky was very foggy the morning of the helicopter ride. About forty minutes into the flight, the pilot lost control. The chopper crashed into the side of a mountain. Kobe, Gigi, and everybody else on board, including two of Gigi's teammates, died immediately in the crash.

Kobe's family and the whole world was devastated by the news. Shaquille O'Neal, now retired, cried. By then, Shaq and Kobe had made peace with each other. LeBron James, who now played on the Los Angeles Lakers, also wept publicly.

The night after Kobe died, thousands gathered outside of the Staples Center—the Lakers' home court—to light candles and mourn the loss of Kobe, his daughter, and their friends. Buildings across Los Angeles County were lit up in purple and yellow—the Lakers' colors.

When Kobe had played his last game at the Staples Center, he still thought he had so much more to do—and so much time to do it. "The challenge . . . is [to] retire and be great at something else," Kobe said. "There's such a life ahead."

On February 24, 2020, over twenty thousand people attended a memorial service for Kobe and his daughter Gigi at the Staples Center.

LeBron James (1984–)

LeBron James was born in Akron, Ohio. Like Kobe, LeBron entered the NBA right from high school.

The day before Kobe died, LeBron passed Kobe on the NBA's all-time leading scoring list. LeBron wrote "Mamba 4 Life" on his sneakers for that game. Kobe had called LeBron to congratulate him and also said, "Continuing to move the game forward. Much respect, my brother." He and Kobe Bryant are considered two of the best basketball players of all time.

41

The date was chosen in honor of Gigi's jersey number two (February is the second month of the year) and Kobe's jersey number twenty-four. Kobe's wife, Vanessa, spoke about her love

for her husband and daughter. She called Kobe the "MVP of girl dads." Beyoncé and Alicia Keys performed. Shaquille O'Neal gave a speech.

Michael Jordan also did. "In the game of basketball, in life, as a parent, Kobe left nothing in the tank. . . . Kobe gave every last ounce of himself to whatever he was doing," Michael said. "Rest in peace, little brother."

Seven months after his death, Kobe Bryant was inducted into the Naismith Memorial Basketball Hall of Fame. His legacy as one of the greatest and most hardworking players of all time will stand forever.

45

Timeline of Kobe Bryant's Life

1978 — Born August 23 in Philadelphia, Pennsylvania

1984 — Moves to Rieti, Italy

1991 — Moves back to Philadelphia, Pennsylvania

1996 — Named High School Player of the Year by *USA Today*

— Chosen as the thirteenth pick in the NBA draft on June 26

1998 — Becomes youngest starter in an NBA All-Star Game on February 8, at just nineteen years old

2000 — Wins first of his five NBA titles with the Los Angeles Lakers

2001 — Marries Vanessa Laine on April 18

2010 — Wins his fifth NBA title on June 17 and is named the Finals MVP

2016 — Scores sixty points in his final NBA game on April 13

2017 — Los Angeles Lakers retire both of his numbers (8 and 24) on December 18

2018 — *Dear Basketball* wins the Academy Award for Best Animated Short Film

2019 — Publishes the first book, *Training Camp*, in The Wizenard Series

2020 — Dies January 26, along with his daughter Gianna, in California

— Inducted into the Basketball Hall of Fame

Timeline of the World

1978 — NASA (National Aeronautics and Space Administration) announces its first group of women astronauts

1985 — The popular comic strip *Calvin and Hobbes* first appears in newspapers around the United States

1989 — The Berlin Wall, which divided East and West Berlin, begins to be torn down

1996 — Major League Soccer (MLS) launches its first season

1997 — Diana, Princess of Wales, dies in a car crash in Paris, France, at the age of thirty-six

2004 — US swimmer Michael Phelps wins his first of six gold medals during the Summer Olympics in Athens, Greece

2005 — YouTube is launched

2007 — Apple introduces the iPhone

2008 — Barack Obama is the first African American elected president of the United States

2015 — Paris Climate Agreement is reached, and 195 countries agree to fight climate change

2019 — Australia endures the most widespread bushfires in history

2020 — A coronavirus pandemic shuts down most of the world—including the NBA season and the 2020 Summer Olympics

Bibliography

*Books for young readers

Bryant, Kobe. *The Mamba Mentality: How I Play.* New York: MCD, 2018.

*Dayton, Connor. *Kobe Bryant: NBA Scoring Sensation.* Chicago: Britannica Educational Publishing, 2015.

Deveney, Sean. *Facing Kobe Bryant: Players Recall the Greatest Basketball Player of His Generation.* Oak Brook, IL: Sports Publishing, 2016.

ESPN. *Kobe Bryant: An Extraordinary Life (1978–2020).* New York: Meredith Corporation, 2020.

Gregory, Sean. "Death of an Icon: The brilliance and the complicated legacy of Kobe Bryant." *Time*, February 10, 2020.

Lazenby, Roland. *Showboat: The Life of Kobe Bryant.* New York: Back Bay Books, 2017.

Los Angeles Times. *Kobe Bryant (1978–2020) Commemorative Issue*. New York: Meredith Corporation, 2020.

YOUR HEADQUARTERS FOR HISTORY

Activities, Mad Libs, and sidesplitting jokes!
Discover the Who HQ books beyond the biographies

Who? What? Where?

Learn more at whohq.com!

Los Angeles Times. ***Kobe: The Storied Career of a Lakers Icon.***
Battle Ground, WA: Pediment Publishing, 2016.

*Savage, Jeff. ***Kobe Bryant. Amazing Athletes.*** Minneapolis:
LernerClassroom, 2010.

Sports Illustrated. ***Kobe: Special Retirement Issue.*** New York:
Time Inc., 2016.

*Uhl, Xina M. ***Kobe Bryant. Sports' Top MVP.*** New York: Rosen
Central, 2018.

Websites

www.granitystudios.com

www.hoophall.com

www.mambasportsacademy.com

www.si.com/vault